DATE DUE

CLAY

Mike Roussel

Illustrated by
Malcolm S. Walker

Craft Projects

CLAY
FABRICS AND YARNS
NATURAL MATERIALS
PAPER AND CARD
SCRAP MATERIALS
WOOD

First published in 1989 by
Wayland (Publishers) Ltd
61 Western Road, Hove
East Sussex BN3 1JD, England

Editor: Hazel Songhurst
Designer: Kudos Services

British Library Cataloguing in
Publication data
Roussel, Mike
    Clay
    1. Pottery. Making. Manuals. For schools.
    I. Title.   II. Walker, Malcolm S. III.
    Series
    738.1
ISBN 1-85210-533-X

Phototypeset by D.P. Press, Sevenoaks, Kent
Printed in Italy by G. Canale & C. S.p.A. Turin
and bound in Belgium by Casterman S.A.

CLAY

Contents

Introduction

Make sure you always handle tools carefully and safely. It is better not to eat or drink when you are working. Wait until you have cleaned up and washed your hands. Clean up carefully after each session. If in doubt about anything, ask an adult to help you.

Caution
Do not put clay water down the sink because it will block the drains. If you leave the clay water to stand for a while, the clay will settle to the bottom and you can then pour off the water.

What is clay?

Clay soil comes out of the ground. It is a heavy soil and is muddy when wet. When it is dry, it hardens and cracks. Water cannot soak through clay. Some people build ponds with a clay lining to keep the water in.

Bricks, tiles and pottery are made of clay fired in a kiln. A kiln is a kind of oven that heats clay up to a very high temperature. People made pottery from clay thousands of years ago. Many of the skills they used are the same today.

What materials can you use?

All the projects in this book can be made with modelling materials other than clay. If you use coloured material, like plasticine, the different colours can be joined and blended together in a very exciting way. You can also use air-hardening and oven-hardening modelling materials, like Das or Fimo. You can decorate and glaze these to give a colourful and glossy finish.

Many schools use New Clay, which is an air-hardening clay that does not need firing. New Clay can be painted with special gloss paint to add a bright, coloured finish.

Real Clay is another air-hardening clay made of pure natural clay. It contains a hardener to strengthen it when dry. You can buy the clay in various colours. If you intend to decorate what you make, you can paint on non-firing glaze colours when the clay is dry. You can also paint on a cold glaze. Real Clay is the best clay to use if you are a beginner.

Tools
You do not need a lot of expensive tools to start with and the list below is a basic list. You can even make some of the tools yourself:
Wooden workboard 60 cm × 40 cm
Plastic tub for water
Sponge
Lolly stick
Knife, fork and spoon
Large, blunt needle stuck in cork for cutting clay when soft (ask an adult to put the needle in)
Knitting needle
Pebble
A pvc apron, which can be made out of a pvc bag and string

For slabwork
Textured cloth or wallpaper to roll clay out on (canvas, hessian, cloth or wallpaper with raised pattern) about 60 cm × 60 cm
Battens (guides)
Wooden rolling pin or piece of broom handle 30 cm long

For decoration
Anything that will make an interesting pattern in the clay surface; for example nuts, bolts, buttons, a thimble.

Reference material
Make a collection of pictures of birds, animals, trees, flowers, buildings, cars, landscapes, faces, interesting patterns and anything else which will help you with details and ideas.

Solid shapes: Make an owl

You will need

- Workboard
- Clay
- Sponge
- Water
- Tools (Modelling tool or lolly stick with one end slightly pointed)
- Decorating tools, including a fork or old toothbrush
- Paints and brushes
- Glaze
- Your own drawing of an owl for reference

If the clay starts to dry and crack, wet your finger and smooth over the cracks until the clay blends together.

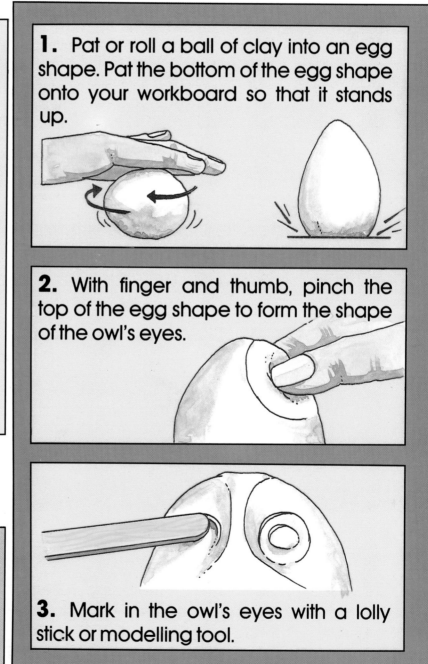

1. Pat or roll a ball of clay into an egg shape. Pat the bottom of the egg shape onto your workboard so that it stands up.

2. With finger and thumb, pinch the top of the egg shape to form the shape of the owl's eyes.

3. Mark in the owl's eyes with a lolly stick or modelling tool.

4. Do not forget to mark the feathers on the front and back with an old toothbrush or fork.

5. When thoroughly dry, paint with colour if you want to. When the paint is dry put on the glaze.

More ideas

Make a candle holder. Pat down a round piece of clay on the work board to make a base. Push your finger carefully into the top to form a hole for the candle (test it is the right size). Smooth with fingers and sponge. Press patterns into the candle holder with a modelling tool. Leave it to dry and then paint before glazing.

Solid shapes: Make a bird

You will need

- Clay tools and equipment
- Your own drawings

How to make slip

Put a lump of clay into a plastic container with a lid. Add water and mix until creamy. Put the lid on and leave the water and clay to soak. You will need to mix the clay and water each time you use the slip.

1. Pinch off a piece of clay the size of a marble for the head. Mould the body shape and pat it down on the work board to make a flat base. Shape the head and beak with your fingers.

2. Score (roughen) the surface of the body with a stick or modelling tool where you are going to fit the head.

3. Slightly wet the surface of the head with your finger and press it down firmly on to the body. Smooth round the joint with a flat tool and your finger. Finish off with a slightly damp sponge.

4. Mark on the eyes and the feathers. Leave to dry. Decorate and glaze.

More ideas

Think of all the different species of birds you can make. Collect pictures of birds and copy the different colours and markings on to your models.

Joining clay

When you join two pieces of clay together it is important that they stick firmly. When the clay is soft and you need only to make a small join, use a little water. To join clay that has dried out but is still pliable you must use slip. Slip is clay mixed with water to make a creamy texture. Roughen the parts to be joined with a stick or scourer. Paint on the slip. Press the parts together and work round the edges with a tool to mix the slip and clay together. Smooth over the joins with your fingers.

Drawing out clay

You will need

- Clay tools and equipment
- Reference pictures

More ideas

Make a duck. Roll out a sausage of clay. Start to draw and shape the head. Shape the body. Lightly mark in feathers with a pointed tool. Mark the eyes and beak. Leave to dry and decorate and glaze.

Make a beaver

Drawing (pulling) clay avoids the need to join it.

1. Roll out a ball of clay and shape the body. Gently draw out the clay from the back to make the tail.

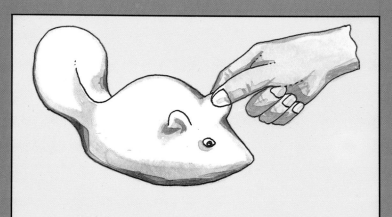

2. Pinch out ears and mark the eyes and mouth.

3. With a modelling tool, press out and mark the webbed feet.

4. Smooth with finger and sponge. Leave to dry and then paint and glaze.

More ideas

Make a swan in the same way but allow for a longer neck. Try making the wings outspread.

Think of making some other animals and birds with long necks, limbs or tails.

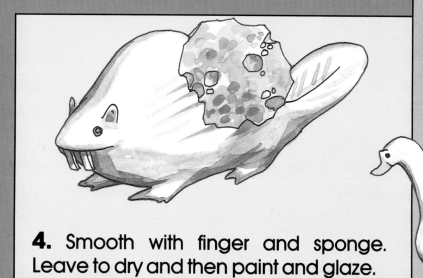

Pinching: Make a pinch pot

You will need

- Clay tools and equipment

Pinch pots are sometimes called thumb pots, as the skill of pressing the thumb into the clay and pinching it between the thumb and forefinger creates the pot shape. Thousands of years ago people used this skill to make pots by moulding them out of a single lump of clay and then leaving them in the sun to harden. Pots were needed for storage.

1. Pat a ball of clay about the size of an egg.
2. Hold the ball in your left hand and press your right thumb gently into the centre of the clay. (If you are left handed, reverse the instructions.)
3. Turn the ball of clay as you press your thumb into it.
4. Pinch the clay between your thumb and forefinger to build the wall of your pot. Be careful not to make the walls too thin nor push your thumb through the base of the pot. Smooth over cracks with your finger.

5. Pat the bottom of your pot down on the workboard to make the base. Smooth over the base, top and sides with your finger or thumb to make a smooth finish and rub a slightly damp sponge over the pot.

6. Decorate by pressing patterns around the sides and leave to dry before glazing.

More ideas

A night-light holder can be made from a pinch pot. Make the pot and leave it to go leather- hard – until it is almost dry. Cut out shapes in the sides with a knife for the night-light candle to shine through.

Add a handle

1. Roll out enough clay to make a handle.

2. Score the ends to be joined and brush slip on to joints.

3. Smooth round the join and rub with sponge.

If the clay becomes too wet leave it alone until it is dry enough to start working with again.

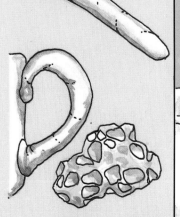

Pinching: Make a piggy bank

You will need

- Two pieces of clay, equal in size
- Clay tools
- Polythene

To join other modelling materials, press the edges of the joins together and smooth over with a modelling tool and your finger.

Decide what size you want your pig. Remember, the surface area of the clay increases as you build your pot.

1. Press out two thumb pots. Check they will fit together neatly.

2. Leave overnight under polythene to go leather-hard. It will then be easier to join the pots with slip. If you are using another kind of modelling material there is no need to leave the pots before joining them.

3. Next day, join the two pots together with slip. Do not forget to score the edges.

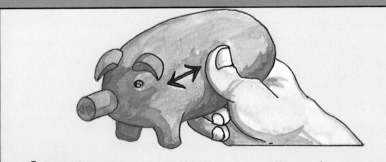

4. Roll out coils to make four feet and a snout and join to the body. Cut two triangles for ears. Join these to the body.
5. Cut a slit in the top for the money to go in. Make it the right size to take a large coin.

More ideas

Using the same method, make an 'egghead' money box. Roll out a coil of clay to go round the middle. Paint, model or mark in a face on the egg. Mark your name on the money box.

6. Smooth over with your thumb, or a pebble and rub the sponge over to clean up. Leave to dry. Paint and glaze.

Slabwork: Make a tile

You will need

- Clay tools and equipment
- Polythene
- Rolling-pin or broom handle
- Battens (guides)
- Textured cloth
- Card template 8 cm × 8 cm

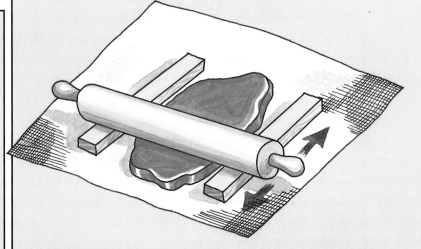

Put the cloth on the workboard and place battens slightly wider than tile will be. Roll out clay to thickness of battens. Peel off and place on workboard. Put template on top and cut round. Press in patterns. Smooth edges with finger and sponge. Cover with polythene to stop warping. Glaze when dry.

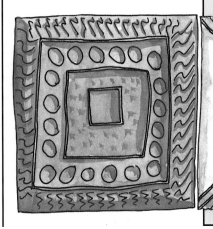

Mosaics

The Greeks and Romans made mosaics by using coloured glass and stone to decorate their walls and floors. You can make mosaics out of clay.

1. Roll out a large slab of clay and cut it into squares 2 cm × 2 cm.

2. When the clay is dry, paint the squares different colours (at least ten each the same). Glaze the squares.

3. Make up a picture or pattern and stick the squares on to a card (a piece about 20 cm × 20 cm) with PVA glue.

More ideas

Why not make a big mosaic, using large and small tiles?

Slabwork: Make a face

You will need

- Clay tools and equipment
- PVA glue
- Reference pictures, or your own drawing of a face

More ideas

Try making faces with different expressions: happy, sad, angry, or frightened. A clown's face would be good, or someone singing, sleeping or yawning. Decorate your faces with clay hats or head-dresses and jewellery.

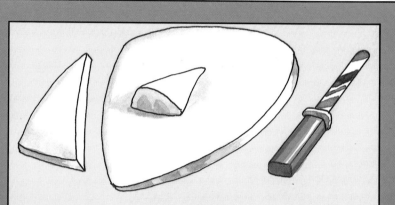

1. Roll out a slab of clay and cut out an oval shape. Shape a nose out of a lump of clay and join it to the face with slip. Press down the edges and smooth over.

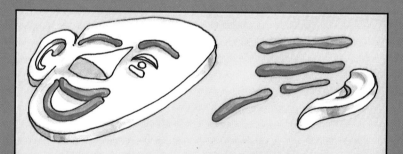

2. Roll out coils for the eyebrows and fix on with slip. Press down the edges. Roll out coils for lips and fix on. Carve out eyes. Press in the clay slightly to make ears or make coils and press them on to the sides.

3. If you leave the face until it is leather-hard, you can then carve features with a modelling tool.

4. When dry, paint the features and add hair. You can make hair by pressing a lump of clay through a wire mesh (old tea strainer), or by glueing on strands of wool. Glaze.

Relief pictures

Make pictures in relief. Roll out a slab of clay and build up a scene. It could be a countryside scene, harbour scene, street scene or any other scene you like.

Moulding clay

You will need

- Clay tools and equipment
- Cardboard tube
- Newspaper
- Sticky tape

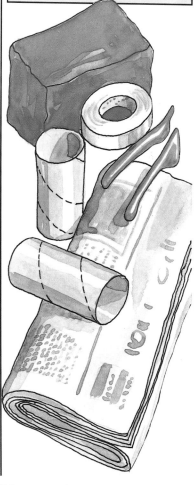

Make a toothbrush holder

join

base

1. Roll out a slab of clay.

2. Tape a piece of newspaper loosely around the cardboard tube. Do not make it too tight as you will want to be able to slide your cardboard tube out easily.

3. Roll your clay slab around the tube. Overlap the clay to make a join. Press down the join and smooth it with your thumb.

4. Cut a round piece of clay to fit the base. Make it slightly larger than the tube base.

5. Join the base to the tube and rub in to seal it. (You do not always have to use slip when clay is soft).

6. Pull out the cardboard tube and the newspaper carefully.

arms

hat

feet

7. Make two feet and roll out two coils for arms. Join these to the body and rub in with tool and finger. Use slip if you want to make sure the joints are firm.

8. Decorate. Draw on features with a modelling tool, add clay lips or a moustache if you like. If you want to add a hat or hair, remember to leave a hole in the top for the toothbrush.

9. Leave to dry, then paint and varnish.

More ideas

Make a pen and pencil holder the same way.
Make a dish using a shallow polystyrene meat or vegetable container as a mould.

Coiling: Make a coil pot

You will need

- Clay tools and equipment
- Polythene

Before the potter's wheel was invented, pots were often made by coiling clay. The pots were fired to make them hard and then used for storing food or water.

More ideas

You can make different types of pots, jugs with handles, bowls and plates. If you want to add handles, make sure you use slip. Putting shape into jugs is not so easy and you will need to practise to get it right. Try adding lids.

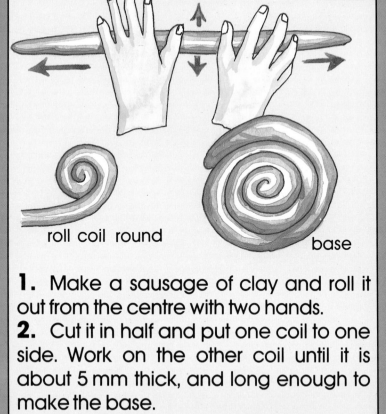

roll coil round   base

1. Make a sausage of clay and roll it out from the centre with two hands.
2. Cut it in half and put one coil to one side. Work on the other coil until it is about 5 mm thick, and long enough to make the base.
3. Start from the centre and roll the coil round and round for the base.

4. Now roll the other coil out until it is long enough to start on the sides. Do not make them too thin. Wind the coils around on top of each other and gently press down. Make three coils. Then use a modelling tool or lolly stick to smooth the coils together on the inside and your finger to mould the clay to a smooth finish.

5. Keep rolling out coils. Build up the sides and mould in the coils until the sides are tall enough. Do not make them too tall the first time.

6. Mould the clay on the outside to get rid of bumps and cracks in the clay. Smooth over with finger, thumb, spoon or pebble.

7. Smooth off any loose clay with a slightly damp sponge.

8. Put the pot to one side under polythene to go leather-hard. At this stage you can smooth out the walls a little more before pressing in the decoration.

9. If you want to leave the coils showing on the outside, just smooth the inside. Leave to dry and glaze.

Coiling: Make a figure

You will need

- Clay tools and equipment

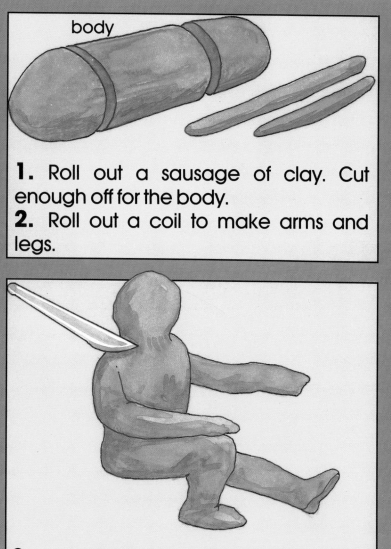

body

1. Roll out a sausage of clay. Cut enough off for the body.
2. Roll out a coil to make arms and legs.

3. Join the arms and legs to the body.
4. Roll out a marble shape for the head. Join to the body.

coil skirt

slab base

5. Make a block of clay for the figure to sit on and join it to a slab base.

6. Mark or add on features. Scrape the clay with an old toothbrush to make hair.

7. Mark in clothes, eg. sleeves, trouser ends, and so on. Details can be painted on when dry. Glaze.

More ideas

Try making a whole family.

You can make different animals by rolling and coiling clay. Try a crocodile, a bear, a fish. Make a zoo or jungle scene.

Coloured modelling material can be blended together in interesting ways. Press together different colours to make exotic birds and animals.

Badges and jewellery

You will need

- Clay equipment and tools
- Large, blunt needle in cork
- Safety pins or brooch backs
- Tape and glue
- Leather thong, shoe laces, ribbon
- Reference pictures or your own drawings
- Tracing paper and scissors

Make a badge or brooch

1. Trace a small picture of a butterfly, animal, car or doll.

2. Mark out the tracing on to card and cut it out to make a template.

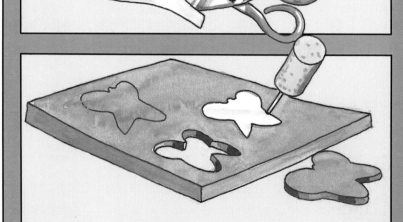

3. Roll out a slab of clay to about 5 mm thick. Place the template on the clay and cut round it using the needle and cork.

4. Smooth and shape and leave to go leather-hard.

5. Carve around your shape to smooth rough areas and leave it to dry. Paint and glaze the front and sides.

6. Glue or tape a safety pin or brooch back to the badge.

More ideas

Make badges for a club or with your favourite popstar's name on them. Make a pendant. Push a hole through the clay big enough to take a ribbon or leather thong.

Make a necklace

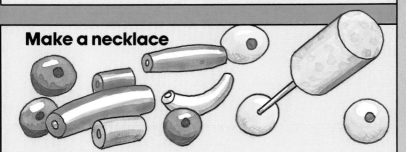

Make beads by rolling small lumps of clay in your hand. They can be different shapes and sizes depending on your design. Push holes through the beads with a blunt needle, ready for threading. Paint and glaze. You can thread the beads on to string while they dry and re-thread on to cotton, ribbon or a leather thong when dry.

Constructing an outdoor kiln

You will need

- 45 house bricks
- 1 metal dustbin lid
- 1 bag of sawdust
- Newspapers
- Matches

This project is intended for adults or children supervised by a responsible adult. Children must **not** build and light a kiln by themselves.

Building the kiln

1. Find a flat space in a garden or a corner of a school field. Lay the first layer of bricks flat on the ground.

2. Next lay the second level with alternative edge bricks as in the illustration.

3. Continue for five levels.

Firing

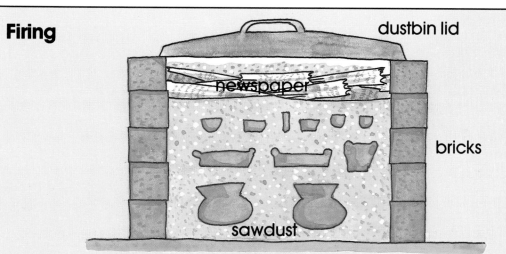

dustbin lid

newspaper

bricks

sawdust

1. Put in a sawdust layer and place the heaviest pots in this layer.

2. Put in a second layer of sawdust and the next heaviest claywork and continue with sawdust and claywork until all items have been loaded.

3. Place some newspaper on the top and cover with sawdust to hold it down.

4. Light the paper and when it is alight put the dustbin lid gently on the top.

Firing claywork in this way turns it black. If claywork is painted with white emulsion before firing, some good pewter effects can result. Before firing, partly dried clay can be burnished by buffing with the back of a spoon or a pebble until it shines. The clay retains the shine during the firing after which it can be polished again. Black shoe polish can also be used to give a shiny finish to claywork after firing.

Warning

Leave your kiln for at least 24 hours so that the pots will cool. The ashes may feel very cold but the pots retain their heat for quite some time.

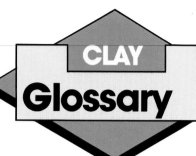

Biscuit (Bisque) Clay that has been fired for the first time to a temperature of 980 – 1000°C.

Burnishing To polish clay at the leather-hard stage with a spoon or a pebble to give it a shine.

Coiling Making pots by building up layers of clay coils one on top of the other.

Fire To bake clay in a kiln to harden it.

Glaze A transparent, glossy coating brushed on to pottery to give it a shiny finish.

Leather-hard Clay that has been partly dried and can still be worked on and joined to other leather-hard clay using slip. Sometimes known as cheese-hard, as cutting it is similar to cutting cheese.

Pinching Making a pot by pinching clay between thumb and finger. These pots are sometimes referred to as thumb pots.

Score To cut, scratch or draw a line on the surface of a material such as clay.

Slabbing Making pottery from rolling out slabs of clay with a rolling pin.

Slip Clay mixed to a creamy mixture with water.

Sponging Cleaning over the surface of claywork with a damp sponge to get a smooth finish.

Template A shape cut out of card, used as a guide for drawing or cutting around.

Notes for parents and teachers

From an early age, children enjoy playing with plasticine, dough and other materials they can feel, mould and shape. Older children can be given the opportunity to develop this natural instinct into an enjoyable, creative activity with encouragement and help at home.

In school, claywork is an ideal craft through which children learn to work together. It stimulates conversation, cooperation and consideration for one another in a group. It is also a personal activity where children can use and develop their creative and imaginative abilities to produce an original piece of work. The practical skills used in claywork complement the other skills being developed as part of the learning process.

Modelmaking can be part of general project work as well as being used in more specific areas of the curriculum, such as language work, mathematics, history and geography.

All the projects in this book, although written for clay, can also be made with other modelling materials. For some children, using plasticine at first will help them to learn the skills of pinching, slabbing and coiling before they move on to different materials and techniques. Working with clay can be introduced in stages, as follows:

Stage 1: Plasticine
Practising the skills of pinching, slabbing and coiling. Making people, models and scenes.

Stage 2: Air-hardening modelling materials
This includes coloured modelling material or modelling material that can be painted and glazed.

Stage 3: Oven-hardening modelling materials
This stage develops the understanding that heat can harden modelling material.

Stage 4: Outdoor sawdust kiln
Making an outdoor kiln and firing pottery in sawdust. At this stage children will be firing clay to higher temperatures.

Stage 5: Using a conventional kiln
Using a conventional kiln that heats up to 980°C for biscuit and 1040°C for glaze firing. You can also, if you wish, fire to biscuit and then paint with a cold glaze. Alternatively fire to biscuit and then add a firing glaze and fire again. Using a kiln in school must conform to health and safety regulations and information and help can be obtained from the County Art Adviser.

Index